E I I   E E   I A E I I   EA   OU
   U I   A O E   IA Y A   E OU   E O

PREDICTING THE NEXT BIG ADVERTISING BREAKTHROUGH
USING A POTENTIALLY DANGEROUS METHOD

DANIEL SCOTT TYSDAL

COTEAU BOOKS

Edited by George Elliot Clarke.
Cover and book design by Duncan Campbell.

Printed and bound in Canada at Gauvin Press.

Library and Archives Canada Cataloguing in Publication

Tysdal, Daniel Scott, 1978-
    Predicting the next big advertising breakthrough using a potentially dangerous method / Daniel Scott Tysdal.

Poems.
ISBN 1-55050-350-2

I. Title.

PS8639.Y84Y74 2006   C811'.6   C2006-903077-4

    2   3   4   5   6   7   8   9   10

2517 Victoria Avenue
Regina, Saskatchewan
Canada   S4P 0T2

Available in Canada and the US from:
Fitzhenry & Whiteside
195 Allstate Parkway
Markham, Ontario
Canada   L3R 4T8

The publisher gratefully acknowledges the financial assistance of the Saskatchewan Arts Board, the Canada Council for the Arts, the Government of Canada through the Book Publishing Industry Development Program (BPIDIP), the Association for the Export of Canadian Books, the Government of Saskatchewan, through the Cultural Industries Development Fund, and the City of Regina Arts Commission, for its publishing program.

for my mom and dad

CONTENTS

I. VIEWS FROM THE GALLERY OF RECENT LIVES

ZOMBIES: A CATALOGUE OF THEIR RETURN

^A The zombies arrive neither to represent the flow of capital nor to join cyborgs and man-eating sharks on the postage stamps recently released to commemorate only the bearable terrors projected across the last one hundred years.

^B The zombies return. Rising up, experts suspect, against moribund comparisons to minds stalled blandly before electronics and coldly burning screens (with looks that barely aspire to the condition of the living dead). Local shop-owners anticipate the promotion of a new clothing line. Senior citizens are thankful for a respite, however pungent, from game shows and Reality TV.

^C After recess, school children are given special assignments and eventually join everyone from army-man 'A' to zealot 'Z' on the now darkening sidewalk with makeshift flags and kazoos through which to breathe an anthem.

^D Managing to navigate a world of only distances – no dawn, really, no day or night – the zombies make their first appearance at the base of the street. A pastor swears that the mouth of hell is overflowing while other rumours ripple from face to face. "Nancy told me some foreigners put a hex on us." "Don't spread lies, Sweetie." "Sorry." "They're only hungry."

^E A theatre-owner lights his marquee with a famous zombie aphorism, "The web will fail before the spider," while an ol' zombie slogan advances unevenly through the crowd: "we are the opposable thumb on the hand of the world thrown from being into the backseat with been!"

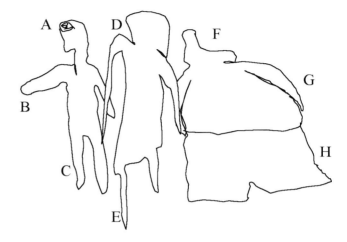

^F And so the zombies dance – leaving everything else to offer up music. Their fissured gaits, the marvelous and decrepit rhythms breaking out around their jaw lines, are hooks upon which a voice is perfectly mangled.

^G Even those who showed up just to watch without pitchforks or torches, even those not dispersed strategically with rifles and well-oiled artillery, realize soon enough that what they have been circled by is their own limit and so circle themselves. The festivities end with a feast.

^H Rumours once abounded in select archeological societies about the accidental destruction of a set of zombie bones. Discovered in the arctic around nineteen-eighty, they predated all originary inhalations. When the ice in which they were preserved thawed, the bones dissolved in a flourish of laughter and moths. Only the dyspepsia of a collapsed star was believed to have been as frail.

PRESERVATION: PERSPECTIVES ON COMMUNITY, MACHINES, LOSS, EPHEMERA, ETC., MOOSE JAW, SK, AUGUST 31, 2004, CORNER OF HIGH AND 2ND AVE. NW AT ABOUT 8A.M., FEELING NOT BAD, WELL, UNABLE TO COMPLAIN, AT THE VERY LEAST MOST SYSTEMS ARE OPERATIONAL AND TRANSMITTING

1. Weather Bureau

the least amount of breeze to qualify as breeze
                                        registered
30% chance of movement from east to west, expect
partial wavering of branches, grey sky that makes flight
palpable, like 10° or something allowing jeans, sleeves, expect later
four puffs of black smoke
as cement truck accelerates,   and hold breath because
sure
        one puff of black smoke won't kill you but a million
will
and though you're not counting or can't keep the proper
rhythm (cadence (

)) or can't remember which digit
goes after which decimation, we have
the technology

that's what a bureau's for, to hold substance accountable
to measurement, a bureau is something that holds you unlike the weather
which is itself an inhabitant of the world. Like the

2. Man About to Fall Off His Bike

. The clouds, for him, so many hands amid hands
that have no idea how to assemble
or associate with fingers. What strikes
his cheeks with speed and dies
was once living with a speed and lift
and defiance. A muscle in his thigh tightens
as seriously as those names
tightened through ink to paper
(before each was slipped small
into the mouth of a clay
monster). The sky is full and soon
he will see where he expected to find
pinecones and grass clippings
only a broken CD remains, and maybe
some grass clippings, but faint in the pavement and dirt as moisture
on eyelashes, and a bolt, too,
busted in its rusting.
                    The predictable whine
of his chain is contiguous with the loose tire of an

3. Empty Stroller

pushed by a woman past past lawnmowers
abandoned together regardless of brand or original
worth, a history of fonts and styles, a museum
witnessing how strong with roars
and purpose certain bodies must have manoeuvred, that smell
she imagines too, not worried about appearing, lost,
that smell of something fresh cut short. And if
                                                    that man
were to have stopped his bike to ask her if she lost
her child, she would have told him
she's taking part in a project at school
designed to teach her the rigours
and responsibilities of adult life, and
if he had asked if she's taking part in a project for school
she would have told him, well,

because she knows that if she were replaced with a DNA-inspired
replica: that little something that is neither mind nor organ, neither
position nor thirst, but is *her* nonetheless would be lacking
and the world changed
                              like if all the photographs were to fall
out of view at once we would lose not just a view but so many flowers
with it (lkie woldrs), like this street which is never the same but always
dreamed in the same direction, always skin before stone. This street
which

4. The Tourist Brochure

calls a street of parking metres and Stanley Cup champions, a street
for citizens who would stop along our serpentine to free
paper boats tangled in Siren-less rocks while ducks newborn peck
at plastic bottles emptied of cola, a street awaiting the fall
of the

5. Man from His Bike

, originally paved to embrace him sprawled out and warning: don't watch
the people waiting on the parked bus while the driver breaks
for a cigarette, don't watch them as though jaguars accounted for
by cages; they're already self-conscious enough,
even when moving, about not going anywhere. But the

6. Aspiring Poet

, in describing the bicycle's journey as ending with a "course spillage,"
does not understand that all loss is not feigned loss and that preservation
is dangerous mostly for the company
it keeps (the best example being the city,

7. Hiroshima

, which those Yanks kept bomb-free for the first campaigns, the buildings
easily lived-through in rising, so as to better understand the repercussions
of their creativity, I mean, in a great flash we burn the skin from a horse
to better later examine why it collides with this and that impediment. The

8. Aspiring Poet

takes the approach of the quasi-agoraphobe in failing to understand
that preservation subtends its own funeral (the

9. Quasi-Agoraphobe

being the one who says: "by not going outside today
I saved x# of ants and kept invisible spores
from death by inhalation"). The

10. Aspiring Poet

is (struck - r) with what the musician told him, "doesn't it (stuck – t)
that you could erase somebody." So: the poet repeats
what Wordsworth said about yellow flowers or clouds
with social anxiety disorder (in a culture
and time before Paxil) or what the two Len'ən/ĭns said about Jesus,
"we're bigger than that." Each

11. Sign

he passes reading his own poems back to him: "this business
operates on the basis of service;" "need a hall
check us out." Each of these poems is the

12. Poster

hanging a few blocks east at the pro-life centre: a foetus in its favourite
and famous position, mute bodyparts circled and labelled to mark potential
growth because this is what we do with what we preserve,
                                                        we circle it,
with the things we must let go, we circle those
too
        ,

13. Our

activity consonant with the activity of the insect knocked
unconscious against teeth, uvula-maimed, another something
down the throat sliding in the slaying

14. And

birth of sums

15. And

dying (

16. But

still surfacing somehow
despite this
                somewhere
with

17. A Speed

18. And

a lift

19. And

defiance

PREDICTING THE NEXT BIG ADVERTISING BREAKTHROUGH
USING A POTENTIALLY DANGEROUS METHOD

"Great harm has been done to us. We have suffered great loss. And in our grief and anger we have found our mission and our moment. Freedom and fear are at war. The advance of human freedom—the great hope of every time—now depends on us. Our nation—this generation—will lift a dark threat of violence from our people and our future. We will rally the world to this cause by our efforts, by our courage, we will not tire, we will not falter, we will not fail."
– George W. Bush

"mists in which human beings once located their own powers, the very powers that had been wrenched from them—but those cloud-enshrouded entities have now been brought down to earth. It is thus the most earthbound aspects of life that have become the most impenetrable and rarefied. The absolute denial of life, in the shape of a fallacious paradise, is no longer projected onto the heavens, but finds its place instead within material life itself. The spectacle is hence a technological version of the exiling of human powers in a 'world beyond'—and the perfection of separation within human beings."
– Guy Debord

What really puzzled Michael Blaine Smith, an unemployed carpenter, was the final frame of the comic strip. The comic was a half-page ad in the back of Fangoria magazine. It detailed the methodology and idiosyncrasies of Andaloosa's Body Modificatering Kit©. In the action of the strip, an average Jane and Joe prepare for a party by adding to their finger foods and cocktails a body (not included with the kit) they have drugged, incised and appended, using the tools and instructions contained in Andaloosa's ll Now Call Now Call Now Call Me Call Now Call Now Call Now

1-800-____-
_____

Phone Now For Free Very Easy And Fast

Body Modificatering Kit©. In the final frame, the average Jane and Joe stand behind a well-stocked table,

tunnel tunnel tunnel tunnel tunnel tunnel tunnel tunne their project bleary-eyed and lackadaisical, its knees to its chest, in a bowl of punch. Michael could not discern if the body was strictly ornamental, or a kind of pungent bullion meant to balance out the too-sweet punch, or something that was not to be simply visually consumed.

The Ab Aeterno Agency's first campaign was a television

commercial meant to demonstrate the bare essence of a foreign car company's newly crafted automobile. The finished spot, a black screen over which a horizontal white line at once snapped like a whip, at once dulled and vibrated, was a success insofar as consumers videotaped and viewed it on their own. The car itself, however, failed. People sketched out the ad's white line over the dark world themselves and used it to pick the kids up after practice and to commute to work despite the bumpy ride and surprisingly poor mileage. lowest we go I promise never lower than this can we be reached

tunnel tunnel tunnel tunnel tunnel tunnel tunnel tunnel
beautifully funtime product promises poem of this indemnity in 5 4 3 2 1 for you and me always very easy for him or her too 5 4 3 2 1 button pushed and that's all how could it get any easier one button we promise how could you fail not to want this tunnel tunnel tunnel tun

Parson, president of the local Chamber of Commerce, and Stan Daley, a life insurance agent, taped everyone—even those with mouths and noses gone golden with gold paint huffed, even the liquor store manager who still lived with his mother, even Mrs. Parson's newborn with the crippled-up fist. Atop each image a voiceover suggested possible plotlines and conflicts (also derived from the raw material of the community). At the end of the film, Annie Knutson, a piano teacher and single mom, read with an image of the town taken from Langley Hill accompanying her: "and this is where the film begins, with you, because none of us has the time or

Of a pesticide someone once wrote: the Phoenix who arose from embers as ash was cast from the air by wind into pieces unwinged and opaque.

A middling community filmed *Introducing the Characters for the Next Big Spielberg Hit* and forwarded it through couriers to Steven himself. The filmmakers, Charles

the money to make it." Upon hearing this, Mr. Spielberg was rumoured to have said: "their project has too much of that other eye which exists within the eye."

Moment (In This Time Depends) / our world is the shape of a great and dark us / it is a rally of material freedom and violence brought / to technological achievement within / the place and time of our powers great powers / powers projected onto this human / world by the absolute spectacle / our exiling perfection located not in those cloud-enshrouded / heavens of future freedom / not in the courage of the has been done / but instead now / within the paradise we own a version of / our generation finds hope in the entities / which will become us / we are their anger / we will advance on every / impenetrable them /from cause to war) / our nation is beyond the earthbound efforts / that have suffered loss grief and separation / that had been human and hence the great and fallacious /threat to our denial of the human / the human itself / its life / once wrenched from life / (no longer of life) / will have but mists of beings / fear and harm have been thus found / by most / we have the aspects of a great /and rarefied people / we lift our earth down at will / most beings tire and falter / fail / we will not

A L L					
		THIS			
	O F		AS PIR E		
				S	TO
COND					
TH E	ITIO N				
		O F MUZ			AK

AN EXPERIMENT IN FORM*

+: It remains trapped in my skull behind a vision of snow falling on cherry blossoms. It remains locked in drawers of reason and doubt. It remains overdressed in a song.

*Author's Note on "an experiment in form": The poem I wanted to write doesn't appear on this page. The poem I wanted to write is an impossibility. (The following words are my attempt at gracefully falling flat on my face.)

+: An absurd fertilization. It would be Moses' burning bush manifesting as paper and ink. It would be the most fulfilling doorway. It would be the entirely poignant, "we are free." The following words are a substitution. A poorly developed Polaroid. A blueprint for a greater machine of human energy.

Reader's Question: Why the apology before the deed? Why the white flag before the declaration of war? Is this what they meant when they said, "modern western insecurity is the ultimate tool of self-defense?"

title(s): girl* sleeping   or
            the one I could not touch   or
            poem   or
            please don't wake up because I feel so beautiful in this silent shadow drenched room

*Author's Note on "girl": A brief character sketch in order to avoid lawsuits, reader assumptions and/or emotional quarrels. She was five feet, eight inches tall. Her mouth looked especially rough. If she were a political structure she would be an empire. If she were a natural phenomenon she would be lightning. If she were a verb she would be "to wish."

*Author's Note on "his words":
This line isn't necessarily true but it is an assumption she often made. Not outwardly but it was present between the lines of our conversation, hidden in glances, buried under laughter, lost slightly in the way she only half smiled when my arm fell playfully around her shoulder.

If she were here right now she would see through his words.* She would say, "you're using this poem to get closer to yourself and further from everything else."

oh ya, he was never her lover

you sleep
like a black & white photograph
at the foot of the bed
like a monochrome still
taken from a chet baker documentary
  close up on his adorable ivory skinned wife

Where is his cloth voice?
Where is his metal horn?
Where is his major rise and
minor fall?

<u>Reader's Question</u>: What is the author implying with the Chet Baker reference?

you sleep motionless alive but dead or the reverse
the shadow cast
by afternoon light sneaking through closed curtains
do not touch you
the breeze does not disturb anything meaningful*

*<u>Author's Note on "meaningful"</u>: I should have added that
  the breeze was caused by an electric fan and that it didn't disturb anything
  unmeaningful on her body either. Also, she was fully clothed and stretched
  out on the floor.

your body

    <u>Reader's Question</u>: Why doesn't the author admit here that he knows nothing about her body and
    never will? Did he forget this poem came with a detailed biography? Did he forget the private life was
    dead? Did he forget his failures have been documented by people other than himself?

more than an advertisement for the impossible purchase

    <u>Reader's Question</u>: Can the author read that last line with a straight face?

or: symptom?

more than a house for the free and clear

    Is he supposed to mention she is only half asleep and
    dreaming of another man? Do you want him to quote the
    other poems he wrote for her, the poems she threw away?
    Do you want him to mention the number of times he barely
    stuttered the lowercase "i" and had her turn him down?

Reader's Question: How about that one?

your body is an experiment in form*
your hands are wingtips   your eyelids veils
your bright skin a brighter mirror

*Author's Note on "your body is ~~an experiment in form~~": I will admit that all bodies are ~~experiments in form~~ but, for the purposes of this poem, her body acts as a 'symbol' for the other bodies. A 'symbol' for the sad body that whispered to me, through cigarette smoke, "you have kind eyes." For the young body in the yellow tank top that ended up puking on the dance floor. For the nude body that pressed his buttocks against my naked thighs and demanded, "harder." For the body that said her prayers. For the body that wrote a poem for me. For the numberless bodies fighting their way through sticky webs of memory to reach the end of this pen.

Reader's Question*: Why did he leave out the bodies he didn't physically encounter? Where did he hide them while he wrote these lines? Where was the body ignited in holocaust? Where was the body passionately entwined in Babylon? Where was the body of Avalon or Eden? Where were the bodies of former ghosts and eventual angels? In other words, where was the body that eternally rises in and out of another body eternally falling in and out of another body eternally rising in and out of another body eternally falling in and out and on and on and on forever?

you sleep   emotionless   alive or dead   or both
that doesn't really matter now
captured in this moment

frozen in a shadow & light & flesh perfection
nothing matters*
not the odour of this room
not my foot fallen asleep beneath your leg
not the higher ordeals you disturb by waking and coughing because

~~her~~

~~his~~

These bodies were on vacation from the Concise Encyclopedia of Poetic Images and Everyday Symbols, the 2nd Canadian Edition, when this poem was written.

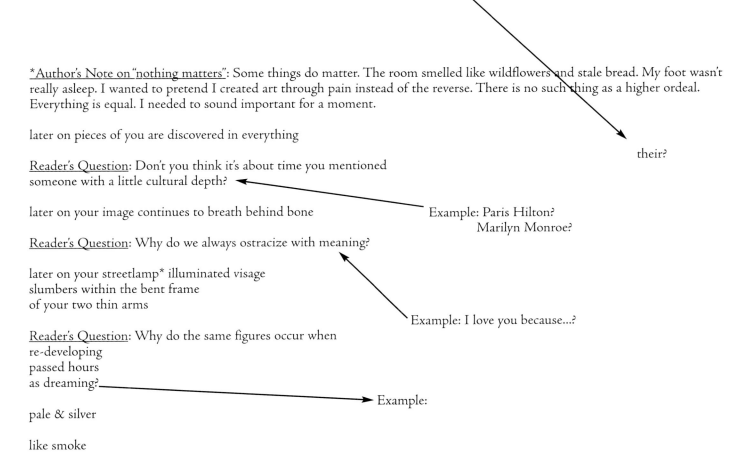

*Author's Note on "nothing matters": Some things do matter. The room smelled like wildflowers and stale bread. My foot wasn't really asleep. I wanted to pretend I created art through pain instead of the reverse. There is no such thing as a higher ordeal. Everything is equal. I needed to sound important for a moment.

later on pieces of you are discovered in everything

their?

Reader's Question: Don't you think it's about time you mentioned someone with a little cultural depth?

later on your image continues to breath behind bone

Example: Paris Hilton?
Marilyn Monroe?

Reader's Question: Why do we always ostracize with meaning?

later on your streetlamp* illuminated visage
slumbers within the bent frame
of your two thin arms

Example: I love you because...?

Reader's Question: Why do the same figures occur when
re-developing
passed hours
as dreaming?

Example:

pale & silver

like smoke

*Author's Note on "streetlamp": This is the same lamplight that cast bogeyman shadows on my childhood dreaming. That lit my dead grandfather's bedroom while we said our prayers together. That forever emblazoned my best friend's intoxicating name-brand bottles. That turned snowflakes into tiny stars. That brightened at dusk. That fell on at least four other bodies and touched each of them in a similarly different way. This is the same light that shattered against all of these poems like glass.

THE TRUE, THE BEAUTIFUL AND THE GOOD: EXCERPTS FROM UNDERGRADUATED ESSAYS

I. The True

The bible was written to be read a million years ago. The bible is meant for even a kick in the stomach from the pterodactyl in the first human gut. The bible we owe so much too. Even stars and prayers, you betchya! Thank you for marking my paper.

Lurking and seriousness of underlying danger is a common value of pesticides and humankind's bodies. For example the mitochondria is the battery of the cell and came from the first woman in Africa. It has help for the lungs and veins. Pesticides lurking and serious as said are changing the "battery of the cell." They give this underlying additives for mutation. The mitochondria needs a new change and adaption to protect itself from pesticides otherwise it will die.

II. The Beautiful

The best way to understand the difference between Kahlo, the Mexican woman who always painted portraits and pain (because she got hurt on a bus plus "the daughter of the revolution"), and the American Warhol (incidentally who got shot) still producing celebrity-ish stills. The best way is an analogy of different incantations of used bullets. Warhol's prints are bulletholes in a windshield happened upon. Although it inspires an initial fascination. It draws attention to places around the windshield. Raising questions like: what exactly constitutioned the drama and apparatus that produced the bullethole? How much external was being involved? But a bulletwound, like Kahlo say in the thigh, her paintings fire us further into what is body.

This poem, all critics agree, is not simply about a bird that is flying in the sky, but the man inside the bird.

III. The Good

The dictionary defines revolution as "any fundamental change or reversal of conditions." The dictionary would not be wrong. So Osaka Bin Laden did not have the right definition of revolution in his mind when he crashed his planes into The World Trade Center Bombings; because though he is a fundamental he didn't "change or reversal of conditions."

Because of globalization, when I surf the internet we all type english, even we listening music, most are english song, and I almost understand, what the music is singing about

METRO

Light against grass along riverbed on an early-twentieth-century morning of grey clouds without rain. Early twentieth-century traffic – its mixture of hoof beats and engines – is audible but not seen. Pedestrians mingle through early twentieth-century gestures and journeys, some hurried and silent, some exchanging words, others seated polite in laughter along the bank. A FATHER and DAUGHTER in the distance walk a path away from us with backs turned in smart attire. The DAUGHTER holds the right sleeve of her FATHER's jacket with her left hand. Traffic quiets. The FATHER and DAUGHTER are before us now though we still only reach them from behind.

FATHER

Do you remember who we are meeting today?

For a few steps, the DAUGHTER contemplates this.

DAUGHTER

I think so, Daddy.

The FATHER stops. The DAUGHTER 's momentum carries her forward a half-step further and her hand pulls away from his sleeve. She turns and looks up at him looking down.

FATHER

Go on then.

DAUGHTER (thinking)

There are the apparitions, the faces, the petals . . . .

The DAUGHTER turns a single fingertip against her chin before pointing.

DAUGHTER (proudly)

And a bough, a bough that's black and wet.

FATHER

You've forgotten someone.

The DAUGHTER's hand drops to her side, fingers white against her coat's purple.

DAUGHTER
Who's that?

Sky-tipped buildings and unlit streetlamps as the FATHER 's palm touches the parted middle of his DAUGHTER 's hair.

FATHER
The crowd, darling.

The traffic is all torsion and nearing.

DAUGHTER
Of course.

Her hand again holds his sleeve.

FATHER
The apparitions and those faces are in . . .

Black.

DAUGHTER
. . . the crowd.

TITLE
In a Station of the Metro

TITLE
Opens Everywhere This Christmas

Strip I

According to these lines,
    when I fell
        it was only twelve thirty-six.
Night club light
    and shadows
        blended in an animated écorché
on Moose Mason's arms tense
    and orderly –
        ready to swell shut
the next set of eyes
    to wander below
        Midge's hairline!
Both
    Dilton Doiley and
        Mr. Weatherbee were bent
myopically over
    screens –
        one was in a separate space trapped
with sightless
    internet
        porn stars,
the other translated furiously
    the cafeteria budget into V.L.T. losses
        and American tobacco.
Insignificantly in the washroom
    there was a splash
        quite unnoticed –
this was my expelled
    gin and tonic
        drowning.

Strip II

The girl
    with the Jughead Jones nose
        offers no reply –
her eyes uneasy
    avoiding mine –
        and waits for the ever effete
Archie Andrews
    to return to her
        (with
umbrellaed drinks
    that fail to urticate any tissue
        or organs when ingested
and are never even
    served
        in a club like this).
Two dance partner
    surfaces,
        more skin
than clothes,
    spy
        over my right shoulder
Reggie Mantle
    in his public desuetude –
        he sucks on ice cubes
and winks poems at himself
    in the back bar mirror
        a few minutes

before closing time.
        Like James Joyce,
                long dead
but still waking,
        he originates
                a language
he knows
        he will never
                truly
see.
        Archie French-kisses
                his girl in the strobelight
while I hold
        their margaritas.
                These words
of mine
        are written,
                calm,
against such loneliness.

Strip III

Though Betty Cooper's $4
        "last call"
                request
for fifty-five cents
        worth of rum
                spills across
the front
        of her silver mini-
                skirt,
other drinks
        will cry
                her long
into the night.
        Other arcanum
                amalgams like poorly lit homes
will partially congeal her love
        because –
                or so the cloud-shaped word balloon
reads above her engilded,
        but never quite
                aureate, locks – somewhere
it is always
        this nighttime
                and somewhere
somebody was born
        on this day
                into this moment

so the bartender
                would always have an excuse
                                to give us something free to decoct
into a new love
                we can only hope in the same bed
                                to pass out with and
inly we
                will never
                                abandon.

Strip IV

Amid Riverdale, at this dreamy hour,
                like a petal of ash
                                upon a filtered stem –
because all of this is transient and drifting –
                I am here tonight
                                writing this poem.
The overall picture this poem sees
                is a field made up of flowers
                                pairing off in twos
and twos;
                and two of its many queries are:
                                What can I do
but want
                each of them?
                                What can I create
while standing here
                alone?

This poem
is the world's seared flakes,
                the dried shreds
                                of the imitations
of life,
                rolled into a cigarette –
                                as smart and real
as an explosive –
                the mind elects to inhale
                                upon lighting.

Strip V

And so Veronica   & Vero na
                na ni ca a pale *sugar*
                                amid (Oh, let's pause
                                                even the music
                                for a second!), maybe, a vortex I beyond the dance
                                floor press myself lips
                first against those anti-vacuous
                                honey honey lips of hers I press
                                                myself not unstilled but
                dreaming

(This page!
          I imagined giving her
                    this page!) as vertiginously I am one
                              shot into an aphelion
                              orbit with ample lonely space
                              to vomit tears and establish an orthography
                    of the infinite cartoon semaphores
composed blindly by
          these bodies draped
                    along with *my candy*
girl in   (Oh let's pause
                    again! (& again!))
                    candy draped these
                              bodies are in the collapsed-
          star rhythms
                    of their movement

Coda

"We're all aphasiacs here,"
                    Riverdale high school's Miss Grundy
                              sweet on my earlobe sighs –
her coffee breath
                    engulfed by marijuana cigarettes
                              and pousse-cafes,
neither of her hands
          wanting
                    to go home alone.
"We're like William Carlos Williams," she adds,
          because she knows
                    that's exactly what I want
to hear (her words being
          that first kiss on the neck
                    that makes everything
but the toes tingle).
          "He invented a variable foot
                    he asphodel-grew
too sick
          to
                    write   .   .
a kind of orgasm
          that isn't
                    to be spent alone.

LYRICS FROM THE UNRELEASED EMO ALBUM
WRITTEN FOR OUR CONVERSATION TODAY

If You're Anything Like My Friend Rochelle

you know the intricacies / of the industries / that depend on you emoting / but what you can't decide / is if you are hungry / or if / you are sad / a world vision commercial should / make you cry but / it doesn't / new shit shouldn't please you / but it always / will / and you should feel better / telling him this / but you don't / and getting up / from the table / you say good bye / whether there is even / a voice / to peel back an affirmation / or whether the room / is as empty as the colour / of burnt coffee calming / the embers / of a burnt town

Whether Addressing the Symptom Proffered or the Disease Feared

whether or not anticipating the day / you will lift your shirt to check your stomach for / a bruise / not / because you've been struck by / anyone in any way / but because you know for once / what you feel inside will manifest / though infinitesimally / as something / that can be held / as though every set of eyes / to turn away / were to brush up against the world / and break out in clouds / that expire crying / like with the cutter / who opens a stable / throbbing / fissure / from his elbow to his wrist / so as simply to say / "i need fixing / here" / you say good bye / through the hallway / through / the hallway / not running your finger along / the clean of the glass / though / you think about it / not wanting to smudge / what on the other side is / in passing / as soothing as the textures / and wet / of what gets eaten / just before / the skin is peeled away / and disposed of

Until One Day You're Left Helpless Standing

in walmart with a partner / from a country so foreign / he doesn't realize / the clerk is paid hourly to take the hand he offers / and really / shake it / while outside / a parking lot awaits / more of what gets parked / the guy pushing carts / one way looks / but the other / no / and telephone wires behind branches / measure out above earth / a horizontal oblivion / of missed calls / wrong numbers / telemarketing schemes / love / love made more supreme / by cell phone towers / from which / (with each "i just called / to say i want you") / emanates an invisible field / magical and rippling / that composes leukemia out of blood cells / in a nearby / body small / with wonder

COHEN

Leonard I'm selling everything I think about to the CBC.
Leonard July 27, 2003, and my student loans are still unpaid.
I wrote a screenplay that will make all the well-lit eyes go misty with glaucoma.
The first line reads: I was raised by Hollywood and grew up wanting to be a Kennedy.
Peter Mansbridge could voice the animated owl with Rex Murphy miming my inflated sense of desperation.
I can no longer stand what Disney is and is not doing to space and time.
Leonard this stained and apologetic misery I chronicle breathes nothing like a revolution.
Leonard our world mapped without any legends is clawing to the end of history one sales pitch at a time.
When will the Prime Minister give homophobes and smokers something to do besides
write letters to the editor?
When will we kneel again to touch the velvet blood drying where Birney's David fell?
When will all these solicitous emails stop trying to get me laid and finally end the human war?
Leonard I systematized a language for a man I met on a street corner mouthing off the
        last four hundred years of Western life. He spoke in that tongue that festers
        unpurchaseably at the edge of living without a home. Everything he uttered I
        phonetically plotted from z to A and back to z and by the end it all just looked
        like screaming, I mean, it all looked just like screaming.
I broke my wrists for the Molson Company but I'm not crying.
Leonard will you still make love to me when I'm old?
You're the closest thing I have to a tradition.
I feel nothing in my bones.
Can we continue donating snow to every under-developed lost cause?
Can we maintain a stony silence on your Yankee mountain?
Louis Riel and I chugged moonshine all the way up the Athabasca and devised a way to
        out burn the war. We're teaming up with Wayne and Walter Gretzky and
        challenging the Republicans to a game of Red Rover on the White House lawn.
Them Republicans them Republicans and them Gretzkys.
Them Republicans in suits always sniffing out strangers. Argh. Them Republicans
        saying, we tried to give 'em suits too but thems strangers wouldn't take 'em.
Leonard just because I use all these proper nouns it does not mean I want to be political.

Just because I sound and smell so Yankee.
Who am I to comply with the universe?
Who am I to drag this corpse around?
There are not enough artists running our hospitals and all these boundaries should emanate light to the point of dissolution.
Leonard I once believed a single line of cacophony held dominion over blossoms.
Leonard my body beats and ensnares itself.
I'm writing a top ten hit.
Come out of retirement and choose me as your second mate.
The first line reads: Leonard I'm selling everything I think about to the CBC.
Come, Leonard, sing with me in your golden voice: July 27, 2003 and my student loans are still unpaid.
Clear your throat, dammit, we've almost touched the final chord.
Leonard our bodies are the broken point on the horizon flashing up between dark and day.
Leonard a voice is always close in the cold and whispers.
Leonard this snow is pure.

ONE WAY OF SHUFFLING IS TEN HOURS INTO BACK-TO-BACK SESSIONS GOING ON TILT*

Another way of
shuffling opens
its mouth
to speak,
but hesitates.

Lights a cigarette.

Another way of
shuffling
reminds me
that "in the
beginning,"

according to
Mike Caro,
the 'mad
genius'
of poker,

"everything was
even
money."

1:1

. There

were
no
odds stacked
against
any
    body.

Every chip
bet
by Adam
brought
the same chip
in return.

Even after
Eve
the bet was still
one-sided
like a
    tail
gripped

loosely
between   its
head's
dull
teeth.

Another way of
shuffling
watches
the world
apple-fall from
the undiff-
erentiated
to the dual

– with
the unveiling
leading
to an immediate
covering up,

with Cain
and
Abel
    peeling

their tear
soaked faces
away

from their
mother's
milky
tit.

These two

faces leaned
in two
opposing
directions.

Janus
syndrome.

And
the odds
were cast out and
multiplied.

And the two
led to
the many.

Another way of
shuffling
calculates why
the house-rules
draw
with a noose's
efficiency

each hand away
from
the feltless,
un
    edged
table of
infinite.

Another way of
shuffling
coaches from
the slot machines

in the sleek
rhythms
of a specialist's

    verse:

*Going on tilt: when a poker player allows his emotions
to disrupt his ability to play.

"never ride
motown
into the flop
unless
there are no
raises off
the button,"

"the odds
are two-twenty
to one
against pocket
bullets."

Another way of
shuffling
names the
word "or"

as the most
notable
exclusion from

the Bible.

I only read
to the end
of chapter five
in Genesis

but I'm sure

the rest
of the book

follows

suit.

A rapturous
'mark'
whispers
to his female
companion

that he wins
a big pot
every time
his cards are
dealt in the
shape of the
number

one.

He says,

"you can't beat
that kind
of destiny."

"Or,"
        I
   think.

Another way of
shuffling
confides:
there is only
one
important
question.

There can be
only one
distinct,
polysemic-
shat
     tering
answer.

Raise.

Or fold.

Janus
syndrome.

Another way of
shuffling
expertly
marks
the deck.

The last way
of shuffling
        (which
        is
        actually
        the
        first).

And yet
another
way
to shuffle
is to
stop
and deal.

Dealing
and shuffling
being
the same
movement
yielding

in opposing
directions.

        A pair

of cards

fall

as my chips

finger-stacked
reach
for that

surveill-
ance-camera-
point in the
ceiling

beneath which
all this
possibility

is conceived.

The rapturous
'mark' informs
his companion:

can be called is
no longer a
hand, just

as
the Way

"the hand that

that can be
named is
no longer the
Way."

and when it has
stopped.

It will be done.

The betting
begins

Raise or fold.

T-SHIRTS OR TOYS: CRIB NOTES FOR A ONE-YEAR-OLD NEPHEW, OR UPON PLAYING WITH JUDE AND TRYING TO AVOID ANOTHER ANXIETY ATTACK

Lesson two, according to my doctor, is to think about T-shirts or toys, something safe. Lesson one is that feeling like I'm water that's forgotten how to turn with the storm into waves and I'm sinking beneath surface, sinking beyond the horizon and shore. Lesson three is that I shouldn't worry about the world that awaits you, Jude, or even what we're going to do for the rest of the night – but passing this ball back and forth is getting pretty old and watching TV will give you ADD, the computer screen cancer, and Heidegger's haunting because he asked questions like, "why is there something rather than nothing?" and how do I even begin to answer to something that vast? And lesson four is that maybe T-shirts aren't so safe considering they're pieced together mostly by hands not much older than yours and never have anything urgent to say. For example: your shirt reads, "Drool Bucket," and there's so much more to you than this. So really lesson one is there are so many lessons I need to teach you before it's too late. Put your ball down and listen close. Your grandpa said the older he gets the more the wind blows directly against his pace no matter which way he's wandering. My own grandfather taken sick to the hospital said – as I held him while he cried – that getting old is no fun. And Jude, I feel old. Like the only substance of this singing is the silence that awaits at the end. Like these bones are the ash of what expired worlds away in a wilderness not yet ready but dying. And who cares if lesson one is what the poet said about that something that with each of us will die? Who cares whether with you and me that something will be the heat from this fireplace, the snapping timber against flame, or what, while holding up the ball, you said in syllables that together just don't work? Because even though lesson one is that Great Grandpa Socrates demanded, "know thyself," what he really meant is make people realize they don't understand what they thought they did. Because even Opa Hegel believed that what he didn't know was as profound as those craters God kneels in the sand when trying to recover, one grain at a time, the

lives he let fall. Which is really just a fancy way of saying there's no need to worry that Uncle Friedrich swore God is dead because when you ask against the abyss "what am I doing here?" your soul is close, with you, that little voice that answers: "I haven't got a freaking clue." Meaning, lesson one is that life is not a game. Life is like the ball you hold out with two hands for me to take: you upright and wobbling, watching me, my palms behind my back motionless in pausing because these rooms are so vast around me that I have no idea what to make with what I am handed. Meaning, lesson two is that there's really only one authentic question, the first question, which nobody's really answered but I'll ask you anyway: "How should we live?" Meaning, lesson three is that the only advice is simply wonder. Wonder that if you and I were a T-shirt whether it would read "Drool Bucket" or "Why is there something rather than everything?" Wonder how only the mobility of dying leads one breathing toward and away from another one, breathing. Wonder that if you and I were deep and original waters if what would be waving is our voices, lifted up upon the tempest of what cannot be said, and what in waiting would hold out a palm for us to break against is the impending shore, and the horizon stripped of light.

SIT, CALM (NOT JUST A BIG 'WHATEVER' BUT SNUG NONETHELESS IN A FEW CHANNELS COUNTING DOWN)

jingles and
the mouths operated by
                              then
theme songs and
                    what is opened
on
   all
this singing
something like
                    imitations
   of innosense, poems
I could've
         have written
when I was like
                    12
                         or
something

the   same
   sitcoms
remain
         after you die
                    only
laughing afresh – if canned –
   for someone else's
fun
you're a game
                    shows
         never
   adjusted them
                    selves

for
because, well,
there is

nothing so
fully
formed as
the reruns
t
v conveys
to children's (x3) children: same
canned
antagonisms alighting
on the   same
obscure laughter
tracked   same
invis
ible
dream of an invis
ible chassé milking the same juicy moon for the perfect characters
insinuated by the perfect gag (the greatest crime never reported is   that
the greatest crime was
never reported (har har har har (UNHEALTHY LAUGHTER

the same plot lined with nothing so
but
insulate
a party with invitations and   that never happened
Like that party no one could show up for because they'd all been shot.

WHAT PRAIRIE POETS DO AND HOW THEY WATCH THE SKY
– for ibi

1

What prairie poets do by accident
is leave the door of the old bus open,
leave the whole damn thing open to fill up
with spring's buzzing flies – so that if you want
to get to your writing (even to poems
about killing flies) you'll have to kill flies
first, one by one, truly coming to terms
with what the wise ones said about sending
the reds and blues of fly guts to fly graves (much
shallower than the hollow that will eventually
hold you).

2

At the end of her email she wonders
what prairie poets do and how they watch
the sky. And for the first time you admit
these sentences you tear in thin strips from
around the half-dead hearts of the creatures
the world coughs up – you admit them as poems.
At last you notice heaving skies surround you
asking what it means to have forgotten
falling bombs after witnessing their sleek
descent; to have misplaced centuries of upturned
eyes, even though these eyes had watched as though
looking up were a home away from one.

3

In an age of messages sped beyond
the limits of distance, the limits of
breath and voice, do not mould atmospheric
lessons. Do not provoke cold premises
through stars for that aching that wanted to
end itself and say: "See! Ache!" Do not kneel
to explain how well the crops are doing.
Do not write poems about horizons hoping
you'll be swallowed inside those bluing heights,
like the painter who copied atop his
canvas the pathed growing into which he crawled
then died.

4

According to most popular legends
the prairie poet is the one for whom
the universe is broken into two:
the half that is ground the way dirt is ground
in the cerise of a blistered popping;
and the other half that is more like air,
neither drawn in nor exhaled, but grasped at;
and the answer to the question "Many
or One?" is most definitely many
plus one – the one that is always one step
ahead as with the horizon pursued
relentlessly but never reached, no set
of last steps striding fast enough to find
their destination.

5

Are the flies that escaped death screaming out
for the rest, who did not, or for more death?
What does the curving of one rainy grey
mean to another grey curving, when
the relation between one and the other
one goes on for infinity until
infinity stops? And the worm atop
soil, writhing in wet – which beaks are most pleased
when it can't stay buried?

6

She forced you away from altercations
with stars, burnt out or forming in spectral-
sized bursts; away from altercations with
addiction and the TV news trial
that kept coasts lost for nights. She forced you
into a struggle with voice, a struggle
with the asphodels and sunflowers of your
speaking – the latter growing a few feet
away from where you sit; the former bloomed
in some purgatory dreamed up centuries
ago by a civilization that
history keeps bringing out to play. She sent
you a name like a warning: to measure
what is – against what you wanted; what you
lost – against what you paid.

7

Squint hard enough and you'll see the sky is every
dead thing vibrating into shimmered blue
smears, so urgent to reach back into sight's
range that every set of senses arrayed
is already dead with that shimmer. Skies
make for these kinds of circling lives. Skies
are made by gods for god-made birds to lift
and circle in, for gods to lift and circle
in, dancer-mad, the few feet of blue
we set aside for their suffering.

8

When you are asked by a friend how you watch
the sky, do you even know which outward
easing of the world to mark out for watching?
Does the sky really arise as nothing
more than the shapes its clouds procure soundly
from moisture amid old winds, from moisture
by sunlight drawn casually out of bugs
overcome by freshly cast spray? The sky
is more than it holds, more than what falls from
sky – retaining all directions, distances
of obsolete distance, the inaudible
in flight.

9

The sky is a sliver under the skin
of all thinking. The sky tries to settle
every conflict by claiming to be
the ultimate refutation of pigments
and easels – the sunset a solution
to problems of light.

10

The sky is not a shape but a duration
of which you are a part of in watching
until your watching stops, and all tendency
with memory fades in fading life, while the sky,
ceaseless, softens away from its origin without
measure unwinding, unwinding away from
its ending as well; that movement in blue
the closest forever comes to bearing up
a trace of all that forever destroys –
of what forever can't hang onto like
this poem you will send her, or the number
of flies you killed without counting them into
the mild stuttering of some counted out
prayer.

GILLMAN: LAST WORDS BEFORE HIS DISSOLUTION

As a monster without a blockbuster film I don't have to be invisible. There's a means for listing dangers so specifically that if you can't phantasize the correlating amphibian . . . . I am the Gillman. Sound it out. A creature and a black lagoon. Gill. Man. Black as the night behind land-tensed gills. As variable and violent as all these oceans and nations composed of much more than men.

Because even if I endeared toward silence in my black lagoon the lungs of another adventurer it was not to increase a count or to draw a body from its name into victimhood. My fins and vertebrae stirred for another's appeasement. My anger, like vows, was conceived. This danger is eel – slippery,

I mean

this danger: danger? Danger. This danger is the decomposition of an inside made outside by a different outside that upon every inside insists; get it? – because the Gillman; because this outsider who loves you, woman, and slays you, man, is the projection of the danger you inflict upon the inside made outside: its woman and its man. This projection. The closest you ever step beyond film.

Because with you there are no spirals, there are no cycles or turns, only fractures that resemble circles in the right distance and opportunity. With you there are only handshakes – the kind formed through fingers brought together by thrown opposable bodies evacuating their collided cars.

I mean, c'mon: the ol' Gillman here's a silhouette, no? Dissolving not from skin to seed-filled core but from the seed to the sialosis – to that hinge where rhythm ceases to be rhythm, breaking on expansion and failing to contract, until only a shaded line remains, please, like bone, with neither marrow for support, nor dirt for a flowered, for a stone-marked vicinity.

Another endangered beast. – ya, sure, sure, I'm a big phony but what's wrong with a rubber suit? – with an oxygen tank hidden behind false fins? Wouldn't you be the same submerged beneath any version of the most ancient waters, flowing as they do away from, then toward, the sea?

The   sea:
On the last day, all waters make known a secret:
the other side of this ocean withholds not a shore, but a steep, unmeasured and equally
misted ocean. It coils up then unfurls against us,
a desperate, more intimate thirst.

II. FOR AS LONG AS THEIR LOOKING LASTS

BOUNDARIES

There's a line of failed instruments the dead will never grieve.
There's a continent nearby growing up in days no headline can surmount.
There's an attention span enveloped by another flickering screen.
There's a drawing of the weapon that will open the end of the world.
Among the poems amid ages (you're looking at one now) are some that will one day no longer be read.
This year a friend's voice will soften, sound, and never resurface.
Time and its sandy shallow bottom,

1 EPIGRAPH + FIVE POSTCARDS ADDRESSED BY AN ADMIRER TO WALTER BENJAMIN
HANGING ON THE FRIDGE + A MEMO ON A NAPKIN (NOT YET SENT)

The letter possesses
a kind of immobilized transiency
that e-mail and, even,
the telephone conversation, erases.
The letter (especially a letter like this that
has travelled such a long, slow distance to
reach you) is a claim
made on the future, a couplet
of claims, actually, unrhymed: the letter
anticipates a future in which its
addressivity will be fulfilled while, at the
same time, shouldering to this projected
space an appropriate message. (Others,
making a third claim, contend that the
letter defines/harnesses/engulfs the future
itself.)

One can imagine the previous declaration
being cast, as a sort of thesis, upon the first
spoken word of the first speaking beast (that
lone syllable long ago adumbrated, from
shivering, wet-leafed coves, against thunder
(an expression that dangled, whole, before
splintering beneath the second resounding
crash));

"every image of the past
that is not recognized by
the present as one of its

or, better yet, to be grasped like
a square of silver paper and folded
into the shapes of still animals, both
mythic and mundane, a malleable
chunk of sky partially grounded by
the augur's mellifluous staff. There is
something here (in the hollow mouth
of a yawning y (propped against
the straight, slight back of
a lowercase b)) not visible
but meant for you, or
not for you but impossibly
visible.

A liminal message – a meaning – in stasis:
forever departing but never finding a way
home: a kind of centurion, the "Angelus
Novus," animated, alive, eyes entangled in the
amassing ruin: a Minotaur, both
furious and doomed (his last howl will mimic
the first howl (that original sound already
mentioned but not wholly
named));

own concerns
threatens to disappear
irretrievably" – Walter
Benjamin

and since I am merely speaking, speaking of the letter as a
chisel subsumed by Today's knowledge of Now, since I merely am, while that same first sound turns over and
over like a worn faceless coin between my cheeks, there must be something hidden in these lines. Not
necessarily buried in the diction, or encrypted in a phrase, but traipsing through the gestures of two syllable
verbs, trapped between the flat edges of an article and a noun, is something like a wounded patient nervous and
breathing, longing to be named by the nurse, admitted, to be called upon and spoken to;

he marks out
with wild, deliberate strides, the measurable labyrinth of time-flattened space that passes between
~~listening~~ me and speaking ~~you~~

AFTER HIS SUICIDE, DISCUSSING MEMORY WITH MY FRIEND,

i.

        Where does
a memory begin? I ask
you.
    With familiar names like Jordan and Tammy? Neil
and Spence? Or with limbs and gestures growing numerous
and foreign as all the letters ever thought, newly
coughed up in a sticky and oceanic soup? ("Take a swim,"
you say, "ha, ha. Drink it up.") In a way

a memory's the reverse of your funeral – you attend
while all those who've gathered are there,
but not; burning you faintly from where the flames
are those rooms, that laughter, these interstices
and eyelashes all fallen beyond dimensions and light,
and the heat is a spectrum of skin you had hoped
to manoeuvre as though watercolours, as though burned
oil.
    "Remember with faith and fear and longing,"
you tell me, "because each of these
is always faith and fear and longing for the wrong waves
with the wrong motion elaborating the wrong boat. And
that's alright for the time
                    being." You lean over my shoulder
as a whisper for me to mouth. Something
about thickening familiarity of whims,
the gradually stilled,

a recollected. You tell me

ii.

                  a memory's like
the crow you found

wandering near the shapes
construction workers carved into their site's earth and open air, this crow

with open wounds in places in the place of feathers, wings broken
into the arms of a gunfighter, bent and elbowed, but unable to
draw. The construction workers glide across gravel. Their
bootsteps and machinery
echoing like tossed stones away from which the crow
cannot take off. The crow walks
a crooked and suspicious   pattern into

dirt. The crow looks accused. From a point way beneath
the stars all these buildings must look
as dumb as bugs flipped onto their backs
and tortured by rising light.
    (But a memory

iii.

does not want to be worked over and decided like: "a crow
without flight is either murdered, or ignored,
or healed." A memory is like the pinprick
origin of the universe,
                              a contracting vigour
more immense than what is least consumable, threatening
always to expand upon exploding.
                        What is here
has to live with what was previously grappled but
never grasped: no fuel is ever felled without a
mouth,
          no falcon's circle widening dissolves
without a centre in the first place
to kill.)

iv.

Where does a memory
begin? you repeat (repeating
me)
          then
answer:

          well,

remember when the eulogy died
and there was no way for us
to write about it?

NOW DEAD THE APOCALYPSE: VARIATION ON TWO MANUSCRIPTS CAUGHT IN THE PURVIEW OF THE MODERN OUTLOOK ON INOCULATION AND SNOW

(1) I

the dark snow then
 come to inoculate time
 the centuries set sleepily on the pane
was again watched

I remember with your friends when the falling
had begun to turn obliquely
to light
and a few feared the window
dwindling
went out into a special camp

they left to journey westward   for him
they had the forces
 The It it
terror
          not horror

and if we are upon He
him it seems
we are to truly be his thousand silver taps

A moral made   ago

enemies are en
emies and flakes are lamplight
against Yes   children

(2) It

farther westward we had drifted every where
on the falling snow on too crooked land falling on every arm and part upon
plain falling part
we went over the barren and Bog were there
softly inoculated there
softly off

Allen wanted spears running upon the lonely waves of dark
Shannon wanted thorns and little crosses to lay out   mutinous
                                        on some old tear
                        the children buried the gate
        and the newspapers and every grandmother wept after us   the camp was right   they cried
it was It
into the treeless dark of the headstones
                        inoculated on
                a polio hacked churchyard   they
remember   see all crying
for Michael Furey and the pile of   he   remember   I
know   I   I I couldn't lay   my little teeth
                                on this general
                        want and the central
It   washaddidn'tdo   I
                                        I
        I   likeman after   he falling
came to what was to come back   a
                were   re   I
        I   the hill of
                                hills and   I
the pile   of arms   thickly

(3) I

forgot the falling and
swooned then
like I never heard their last shot was
the descent
through his slowly realised never
faintly falling
 like with the soul and I
I forget to want it
to want like faintly
shot universe
he
as I   of end   wassnow

(4)   ,

        .   ,
          ,   .
                    ,   .
          ,
                ,
        ,   ,
                  .
,.   ,   ,,   , .   :   . . .

(5) and

 all diamond upon my forehead
the dead
a bullet right through the living

Dublin-Vietnam (1907/1979)

"Not wanting to leave his family to join the combat, _____'s husband held his wife's wrist while three rebel youths struggled to kidnap him. His grip finally gave, but, _____'s children report, their mother discovered a miraculous impression of her husband's fingerprint on her wrist, an impression that remained indefinitely. Months after the fighting had ended, _____'s husband was rumoured dead. She told her children she would use this fingerprint to recover his body for proper burial. Her husband's body, however, was never recovered. _____, with her strange impression, also never returned."

> – Nicolas J. Frank, "Private Life of a Skirmish: 'Many Who Survived the War Were Still Lost to It,'" *Harpers Magazine*, January 2002, p 67

In a Local Legend

He, disappearing, touches her. She searches out later this same touch.

In a Short Story

as the man withdraws from
the woman he reaches
his hand out but catches
only her wrist instead with such
force that against her skin
his fingerprint
is visible in remaining

the woman later
struggles within
a limb-filled pit while searching out
his hand and pressing
each blood-muddied print
for verification beside
the print he formed against her

(the particulars of the man's withdrawal could range: from his body dragged back-first into a hole newly opened in the earth to his veritable re-trenching at the leather-gloved palms of quarrelsome soldiers armed and gritty: from his transubstantiation into cedar to his dissolution in a kitchen appliance for the sake of hungry guests)

In a Novel

the same two individuated episodes are miniscule frosty apparitions on a larger frozen window upon which is etched a vast history of the distant planets themselves becoming gulags and the constellations becoming surveillance regimes beneath which certain protagonists churn out heartwarming musings against this watching and insofar as there remain no vistas in the sky unoccupied the meeting between his fingerprint and her wrist is nothing more than a single infrared sight in a multifarious millennial assault nothing more than a pair of links in the chains winding round these bodies enclaved from system to system

In an Animated Film

the imprint is anthropomorphized and songed without making visible the face at the tip of the wrist or the body at the end of the hand
followed intimately with a gendered voiceover

In a Gallery

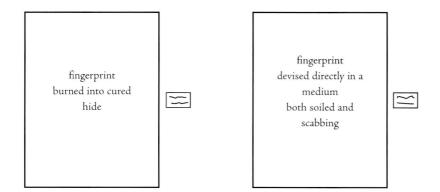

fingerprint
burned into cured
hide

fingerprint
devised directly in a
medium
both soiled and
scabbing

In Her Dream

like people from your childhood

                                     a massacre's that
                             faint.
                            in a trench,
                                         I didn't know

                            Which hands were yours?

FACES OF BUKKAKE 6

begin by watching
the face immediately

not the forty-seven men naked
though normally diffuse
together drawn
the way ink seeping
to the end of a brush

though usually

diffuse is drawn
as a single stroke when
touched at last to
a moist page

the only angles entirely
uncovered for the cameras are
the woman's

most of the men
that surround her
have not removed
their socks

begin therefore
by watching the woman
from where
she exhibits herself with
well-timed blinking

for though pinned
to the centre of the room her
face
is to this encounter
what fragrant and gilded
strings are to an extravagant
marionette
(as though the terrain
beyond the cameras
and men
was the surface of a mirror
in front of which
the woman solicits
with vanquished and
pedestrian care
the prechiselled and
ancient moulds

of reclining marble
and projects
(as a crowded wave
projects
a pallid foam)
  her kneeling self
  her lid-silenced gaze
  the patient and hungry lip of a funnels open mouth
  wavering beneath her chin
  her unchipped dentition offered up
  hieratically for preservation through
  received magnetic signals)

the woman's face
as these socked
and circled men
encounter it
is nothing more than
a face

meaning
a)   her face is analogous
to the protracted handshake that conveys much more
than an innocent greeting
and
b) her face is without
a grammar

since jargon in such cases
is inevitable (requiring a certain
skill and
timing)
each man extends his body's most
articulate and private
voice discernable first
through the distinction left or right
then through a proliferation
of styles

the classic jackhammer pound the
three-fingered caress
the pinkie to tip

backhanded waltz   (one two three
four one two three four)
and
less regularly

the bare hips
thrust against
a motionless and
half-opened   one two three
one

two one

one

these are the recalcitrant rhythms
of a traversal shaded against
the plenary constellations
of the face

the mute acrobatics
of the new dead risen curious
and only half
awake as they tumble away from
the circle's edge

they take turns doing this

stepping forward before
fading into the crowd
of other apparitions haunting
the two-dimensional home
of future television screens
with a particular repeatable
movement housed
in a particular repeatable desire

since all

labyrinthine resolutions
remain as impenetrable
and singularly populated
as the first

the video cassette's cardboard box
will contain an anecdote about
stripped ephebes tossing back
to ariadne
her own string

the box
will warn

there can be no more kissing
one another to sleep
with couplets
no more
than this sequence
of fixed forms

the woman will raise
the plastic funnel
above her face
pull a latch
engulf through
rubber tubing
the air-cooled fluid
as though
she were drawing life
from a shallow well
grown thick and
waterless
with
pennies

but not

yet

the men
remain crowded

into the anonymous room
alone

they are cumming

and they are going
to cum

the woman sits

on her folded

lower

limbs

ALPINO. (2002)

Which of the old masters knew Guernica best? Goya scratching out lines on the shield of the page like a farmer scribbling knife-sharpened-pencil arithmetic on the barn wall? Picasso unfolding antique vases into the shape of tormented mouths?

Arroyo floating cartoon bombers like Questions like this are repeated, eye-framed frame, in a mode that masters knew Kennedy best? Which Richard? Did Marilyn herself, as she letter x? Behind my vision's wall *Art So Different, So Appealing?* plays to an Hamilton and Independent Group

Browning, Robert. "Fra Lippo Lippi." *Robert Browning: A Critical Edition of the Major Works.* Ed. Adam Roberts. Oxford: Oxford UP, 1997. 174-83. Caws, Mary Ann. "A Double Reading by Design." *Journal of Aesthetics and Art Criticism* 41 (1983): 323-30. Fisher, John. "Entitling." *Critical Inquiry* 11 (1988): 286-98. *Pop Impressions: Europe/USA.* Ed. Jasmine Moorhead. New York: MOMA, 1999. Mitchell, W.J.T. *Picture Theory: Essays on Verbal and Visual Representation.* Chicago: Chicago UP, 1994.

balloons above the earth's dull face? though slightly manipulated by every pre-dates Puff Daddy. Which of the old of them knew Marilyn? Did Andy? Did unwrote her signature poses with the Material Reality, or *What Makes Pop* auditorium of movie posters. Richard played by next year's Oscar winners.

Marlon Brando as Jasper Johns shouting a monochrome Yankee flag against abstract spatterings of lamplight, black and red Malevich rooftops, Clement Greenburg constellations. An Andy Warhol impersonator (the pre-condition for a Pop exhibit / the theatricality advertised and foretold by the surface of the first transferred images) slithers through the gallery wearing a wig silver as the text-filled, metallic saucers that precede each section of the exhibit like glimmering "in the beginning[s]." Patrons and tourists alike employ the word "you" when addressing the less-than-a-replica-but-more-than-a-photocopy Andy the way

parents and children ask trip?" Andy and Andy, walls of a collapsed lung, replies to a question I in my surroundings

the Santa Claus at the local mall if "your reindeer are ready for the even Andy and Santa Claus, are as indistinguishable as the opposing the limbs of lovers 69 bound in a candle lit room. "Originally," he never asked, "I wanted to do abstract like Pollock but I decided to indulge instead of the reverse. (*chuckle*) Whatever that means." Which of

the old masters knew Andy best? The curator? The actor? The nuclear family? Me? Which sequence of soup cans is piled directly beneath the sublime? How did Robert Indiana know when he was done making "Love?" Andy whispers, "go, six months hence. I'll have reprinted Goya's sketch of the World Trade Center Bombing on empty cereal boxes." I regularly peer over your shoulder longing for the actor playing me to walk through the door.   Dan S 24/100

AFTER HAVING SOMEHOW FORGOTTEN YOU DIED THEN BEING TOLD AGAIN

For the Speed of Tumour

before recalling your name
he says:
a book about physics:
                            says: light's
speed is slowing
in time
like everything
: he mentions you and this is the how of i remember you but not the why or it's the when
and the where but not really the what of keeping up: "slower
than my tumour": that's what your eyelids blinked like animal become
limb in metal teeth gnashed:

the tumour awaits in all twelve dimensions: not as a buyer for a new nestling but: faint
like those kingdoms in stories so impossible they're mist: throbbing only as a pulse
of shear glass for an inhabitant

                    falling ()

                                                    from height
                                                            he
says:
einstein's cats   while their master
scratching and scratching   solved the problem of a universe
                    to get out

For Imagination and Memory

a professor of mine is troubled by the imagination because once with the path
he walked late in the snow, walked already for him by others gone by also, both early
and late, he among them, having previously trailed out a direction for himself, he
imagined:

this path my grandfather's insides, hospitalized for
is the scar 'spraying' without protection, couldn't
along the base properly expel excrement (organs more cancer
of a breast than guts). what was prescribed made a russet
running free storm behind him. on his hospital bed on his
from the side. not fired because not aimed. not exposed
danger because uncovered. all over the wall. away
of what from fragrant thrown. not buried because never
was dangerous in cured
spreading

For What the Birds on the Other Side of this Glass Should Amount To

no more of   what was down can be lifted up

the paths birds above the buildings release should
remain
in the sky, a new
distance like jet stream, a new cloud to trail
floating in the 'where they'd been,' a new accumulation freeing miracle up a new
rain and
by god a new growth

For Yesterday into Today

ignore what the ancients said about one voice for every body or
light being that place death warms and
sputters into a sighed burst of honey

every death is its own voice without a corresponding set of ears
breathing is as stars thrown away
                                        by light   vigour
of morning where all deep wells were flattened against
thirst

For Miracle

you comfort your mother as you die when she tries to comfort you

after your second operation you are blind but no one knows until you are handed what
smells of sage and inhale, run fingertip along smooth's edge

a thumbs-up slows in photos from my cousin's wedding

during practicum collapse
with brain tumour
to knees

make masks for an art class so long ago, on my farm,

in a hallway
of the school that still stands and makes trouble without you
walk
walk footsteps that must be sea shells echoing the oceans of our greater forever
all along traveling immeasurably
our
counted down

though your mother tried to comfort you as you died you comforted her confronting
death   he
tells me this
says:

"miraculous"

For this Morning

coop   coop   door   coop   door   coop   coop

fence   turkeys   fence

    turkeys

fence   turkeys   fence

    FOOD

fence   WATER   fence

    turkeys

fence   turkeys   fence

plasticfence   fence
stuck   me
  infence   fence

           my mom

fen fence   fence
ce
  fence   fence   fence   door fence   fence   fence

chirping on morning blown away. i say: amazing, the wind sounds so cold but it feels warm. plastic stuck in snaps and elating. my mom says: it always sounds that way through a page wire fence.

For What Light Amounts To

SELF-PORTRAIT AS MINIMALIST

.

, he said,
drawing away from silence as from a bath emptied of a comatose boy, he
said, a bath gone all inky like coaled with overworked limbs,
underpaid and earnest about
moving north
or south, to the cabin maybe or simply out, the water peeling in sinewy
sheets away from the lifted but rising-no-further shoulders,
he said, drawing away from
silence like that is like a breath drawing
ash out of this
cigarette,
,
drawing silence out to that edge of the fenced-in dugout where the trout can't
help but escape when the flood finally comes, he said
like
you get it? where I'm coming from?

. .

because where we do not speak, the world at least,
faintly signals he said, not in your place, but at your place,
the one set only after dinner
has been served
but never eaten he said, tracing
byways as rivulets on that wife's skin, he said,
fat man's puffing thirsty
between sentences is
the lowest degree of resemblance
between mouth and ear required, he said, for
you to   , be
        sure   , he said,   ,
he said,   ,   ,
                        ,

. . .

he said silence
                is water because it's
                        always flowing through this
and that everything like some
matter from
                space, he said, visible through calculations nobody here can
  decipher   , he said,
water is ordinary
like a chair
                you curl up in
                                and
petrify

THE TRACT WHICH BORE PROLEPTICALLY THE FOOTAGE (A CHANGE IN OUR RESCUE STRATEGY)

9.11   It is no longer enough to be bound by what we witness.

9.1   The footage is something like this.

9   Something so obvious as not to acquire the practical inscription of the words that could have passed from _____ _____ to (   )

8.1   The footage is a ladder etc.

8   From above the city, it casts a runged shadow on rooftops and streets already shadowed between and beneath all this towering

7.21   You and the footage are not a tautology.

7.2   Nor do you enact to the point of stasis and vacuity the teleology of a tautology.

7.1   Nor do you tautologize the teleological stasio-vacuosis of the point enacted etc.

7.   Etc.

6.2   The footage neither reflects nor projects the world.

6.111   As though faint entrails, knelt over and picked through,

6.11   as though a vacant skyline for the augur to rechart,

6.1   the footage and its looping at last refract a world.

6   To respond ethically means nothing more than being even partially worthy of inhaling within this difference.

5.4   Headlines gather most easily around the footage and read:

5.3   Unmanicured Pieces of Processed World in Manicured Patterns of the Footage

4.21   The limit is that part of seeing around which the footage loops.

4.2   Limit labels seeing with the words: rewind, repeat, obsessive return eternalized, free/unfree association.

4.1   Seeing moulds limit into the self-consuming stitch that draws together the footage and that from which it was supposed to have been split.

4   That annumerical pre-eminent affect of another reverse affect – pre-eminent. Annumerical.

3.11   The gap is the limit that makes: "footage like this."

3.1   Makes: "There is something about footage like this."

5.2   The Footage Is More than an Icon: Speaking as It Does of More than Itself

5.1   As Contestants in a Changed World We Are Never Seen in Profile but Met Head-On Like the Footage Bearing Yesterday's Answer in the Form of a Question

5   The Mirror that Looked Back as though a Reflection Is Not the Footage (the Tract which Bore Proleptically the Footage Is Not the Mirror)

2.21 Whereof one cannot see, thereof one must pause the footage.

2.2 The pause is determined by a gap in the skyline.

2.1 Whereof one cannot pause, thereof one must see the footage.

2 The seeing without pause must also meet the gap.

3 The gap is the limit in "footage like this" that has only ever wanted to make you afraid of yourself.

1.112 The footage is a succession of pictures.

1.11   Analogy is to this succession of pictures
        what ruins are to the lives within which the
        footage is rapt and unextinguished

1.111   Each deferring to the next, the pictures are
        arranged like bodies plummeting along
        a line without music.

1.1   (along with singular repeated sounds.

1   (along with repeated sounds resounding)).

0.0   What I mean is:

0   "it's like a movie."

HOW WE KNOW WE ARE BEING ADDRESSED BY THE MAN WHO SHOT HIMSELF ONLINE

"We never knew his fantastic head"
– Rainer Maria Rilke,
"Archaic Torso of Apollo"

I. How We Know We Are Being Addressed

Not because misbegotten clichés are the surest.
Nor because there is no other choice (though that

sounds right). No. Not because with only a sound,
a well-played gesture, he in his silence embodies

what films have hoped to raise a profit on through
malformed skeletal structures and obscure flesh

(making what is meaningless and unfathomable
more unfathomable but less meaningless through

counted bodies disposed of at the end of each
scene). How we know the man who shot himself

online is addressing us. Not because of the endless
iterability of his movements – the way we can

break them into bits, re-watch them again. Not
simply because light's multiple sources fail

always to light the same corner (fail to stop us in
those films from trying to escape from the main

floor to the basement when we're chased). Have
you ever received a message from someone who

doesn't know what they're capable of? We don't
know what we are capable of. Immediately,

the world is no longer the calculus of opinion
and pose. Immediately the semblance of a seeing

as detachable from the seen, as a blind eye from
brail, is no longer nurtured, is forced to pull

its own weight. We know the man addresses us.
The world is now only we, who are not the man,

and the man, who is. Setting known against not
known. Setting known against what we're capable

of.

II. The Man who Shot Himself Online

Chair's creaking
through inaudible
talking. The heavy
sound of objects heavy
against table.

after

pause:

Then.

Sniffling. Cell phone
dialled. Down
    the hall, inaudible
talking. Down   hall.
    A door. Audible.

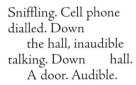
Thank you. Here

ya go,
         Senior.
Water,

after

      pause:

some more.

Ah

fuck.
    Where'd he get
it?   Nobody

 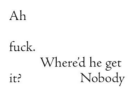 

            shook
him.
Holy fuck.
          Dammit. Ah
fuck. Sigh

                    .
                    Dammit.
Sigh. Blood trickles

the concrete

          . The concrete

gathers

          trickling.

III. How

A man walks into a room with a gun in his belt. A man with a gun in his belt takes one last drink of

water. A man with a gun might wonder which far off glacier that water was rescued from. He

wonders: which oceaned light pale with morning. A man in a room mimics the magician who

claimed he could put multiple bullets in his head – not realizing the magician's trick was to

simply place the shells in his mouth to the sound of applause and surprised laughter. A man walks

into a room for questioning: maybe the man misused the photographs of small children; maybe

he surreptitiously paid two baseball teams to lose the same game and they played on and on for

weeks; maybe he doesn't want to go home. A man walks into a room having given up his dream of

piloting the first wave of troops to the sun. A man walks into a room to count the paces from here to

there; to try out the shirt his cousin gave him; to test the defiance and vitality of what feels and

thinks.
A man with a few friends hungry for a poem

about a man who puts a bullet in his head walks
into a room in a really believable MPEG. A man

who wants to read a poem about his head pulls the
trigger. The poem about the man hopes to do the

same. The poem hopes to put the world right in
the same way. A man walks into the dementia of a

room around a walking in man. The steel-filled
sweating grip of a seated man. A barrel's acute

storm disperses.

IV. How We Know

We know the man through our greatest danger.
Our greatest danger is to know the man levelled

into the two dimensions of the man who shot
himself online. Levelled into this homogeny

as continuous as the prairie seen from a plane –
with sown hectares measurable by thumbs, with

patterns that excite our themes of domination and
failure but never impel us burning to earth. The

man impels us burning. What is knowable in the
man who shot himself in the head withdraws

from knowing as a turned cheek withdraws from
the knowledge of that next terrible blow. What

needs to be known in the man speaks as languages
archaic and ancient speak, seeming so foreign

and new but in truth chattered daily in a distorted
form. That originary emergence, emerging

still always foreign and undistorted. That oldness
underneath speaking. The advice of every death

is watch not the dying but the dying's watching.
Watch not the event but that which in the event is

watching back. If we don't buy that, at least buy
this. Buy this: Learning to live is learning to die.

But learning to die is not learning to live. The first
great joke that every treasured story, in its

snickering, kept from us.

V. The Man

VI. The Man Addressed

I knew him enough to say I knew him. Would I have done anything differently? I wouldn't have

let him leave so young. That's nothing. I think it's a symptom, really, of the movement of death from

the home to the hospital. I think you should think of this as circles decreasing around a vanishing

centre. Sometimes a refusal keeps time with a turning back. Once I felt like saying something.

Ya, he said stuff to me about it. He said he was never coming back. And he had no reason to

come back. When I first saw him I could never have imagined him thinking of doing such a thing.

No idea. The first time I watched the tape, I thought he was going to pop the officer. Me too. I

know I would've. What's the big deal? Seen worse. Like you saw on the tape, I left the room

for a second time at 10:47, heard the shot, returned and found him dead. I thought

somebody'd shook him down. And somebody after me will ask: what do you offer the guest

stepping in from the night in silence? I didn't shake him down. What do you offer the guest

stepping in from the night in the completeness of silence? I couldn't really watch it a second time.

VII. How We Know We Are Being

When we stop worrying what to place over the place left for us by what left us. And maybe our bones. Stop looking for pieces of our assorted and abandoned ribs and femurs to fasten together – to

keep us busy for a century at best with questions. With the only questions at best being: would any

of the new nations know how to sponsor this? Would any company know how to market what

we mended? Break the promise our cheerfulness made with itself. Break our habit of not believing

what is not believable. What mortar must feel in so precisely unfastening the moorings of the last

bridge to the last town with the last set of legs for leaving. What mortar must feel to remain mortar.

Expose this. The world ended in a line of newspaper around seventy-five years ago. The

world died in a poem spoken millennia away from being written down. In this call to change, we

dream against what forgetting judged best to remember. We dream in time with the refusal that

keeps time with the turning back. We dream away our cheerfulness in the bed we forgot to make

between speaking and speaking before.

VIII. We Know We

Otherwise there is no distance between crown and king. No rapport between our choking and the

partially swallowed bone now lodged in our throat. Otherwise the depths beyond those

canyons we could never scale are themselves conceived as floors for the ornaments of strolling.

If all that matters is what happens between and then with a straight face we could say, "neat." With a straight face we could make a number-one-hit screeching "Que Sera

Sera." For a laugh we could argue that death is not the beginning's outside but the outside of ending

and that what is between our first and only grasp and, at last, the release, is happenstance,

"somebody else's problem," . Other wise. If what matters

IX. Addressed Online

http://www.stileproject.com/dec-2004.html

X. Addressed by the Man

Once the gaze of a fantastic head we never knew
was enough. Once this fantastic and sculpted

head, lost to history not as mountains are lost to
wind's torsion, not as peoples are lost

to "oh well." This was enough. For through the
sculpted torso glowing this gaze glowed,

this glow a fragment watching not as an ethereal
relative, kin, but as a hard fact of nothing where

something was – could still be – but in its stillness
was only what signalling is in its faintest dream.

Once, this gaze could watch with the diaphanous
glisten of a predator's shoulder, with the ripened

thought of an effaced moan – this fragment in
seeing could shout without not seeing you in all

your acrobatics, could scream without ever
stopping to blink: "you must change your life."

Now, the head is whole. Now the man's head is
almost whole and not sculpted – not sculpted

as perfect as the edge of an exploding star, not
dazzling in slight twists. But even still,

from the man's head's partial beyond – unseen,
like prayer, unseen, like hands together

in prayer before closed eyes – this nothing where
something *is* watches; this other we, missing,

enduringly entreat in their brief oblation, in the
gaze of a fantastic head we never, in this head-

sculpted loss – the message is the same – (repeat)
change.

GHOSTS: SOME EXTRACTS FROM THEIR EDGE

[17] Now, the tradition of rooms has always essentially been to ensnare ghosts. A domicile not in possession of one unravels – a new language going uncharitably mad against ears. We could recline in such a space for all centuries and between howling and naps never catch a glimpse of ourselves, or one another. For if we only ever mingle in bedsheets, ghosts are the two ovals sliced away to make room briefly for eyes.

– from a footnote –

"Neither ghosts before enclosures nor enclosures before ghosts." "The shared and pale heritage of lakes and of forests recommences in the hall closet." "Everything retires with ease into the same scars." "Listen – like a pair of trim and marooned talons a ghost settles as faintly on the corniced rooftop as in snow."

– from two textbooks –
and two poems

– from Lessons for a Child Who Wants to Be a Ghost –

. . . Slowly, move this way: anything in the corridor, within your reach, near buried, is feeble as the tiny bones of a deaf ear . . . Only passing through forever: as though the first line to begin curving away from sight were also the last to remain visible without falling into . . . Early on: you get a lot of mythological apparatus, but you know your fire is authentic if no one can even move the ashes in the morning . . . This reassembled outside: beyond conditions and erosion . . . And accumulated worth: if you land somewhere frozen act surprised to find a single grasshopper struggling at your feet . . .

Do ghosts pervade either side of a threshold or subsist at the tip of its dissolution? _____
_____
_____

Do the anthropomorphized creatures on
– from an entry level exam –

– from an interlude –

My Korean friend claims she always tucked her chair in as a child. A classmate had warned her that any seat left drawn away from its desk would be taken up immediately by a ghost. In near silence, this apparition would repeat the gestures of the chair's most recent occupant – for hours into the night, with absolute fidelity to the original's momentum.

Beneath pavement, sneakers exhale hands here – stitching. A dictionary opened on the table lists dotterel just below dodo because they are members of the same age.

– hints –

Other acquaintances have professed a similar fear of steering wheels, remote controls, etc.

– from miscellaneous –
communications

There is
nothing but
a s h a p e
inside what
is missing.

Lives and
n a m e s
combine to
r e a c h
i t s e d g e .

the photographs
taken of them
and the cartoons
some of them
scribbled in their
math notes and
the stories the
families   tell

and   all   the
rooms   main-
tained with the
same CDs in the
stereo and the
clothes   still
spread dirty on
the floor and all

The Poster

a reverse piper

calling
them closer

There are
points

beyond   in
the ether

twinkling

faint

and

opaque

their   postered
eyes staring in
on the world
from the outside
asking   to   be
found in the
p h o t o g r a p h s
taken of them

and the cartoons
some of them
scribbled in their
math notes and
the stories the
families tell and
all   the
r   o   o   m   s

but   not
all the way
h o m e .

Though un-
perceivable
without   us

they cannot
be reached.

maintained with
the same CDs in
the stereo and
the clothes still
spread dirty on
the floor and all
their   postered
eyes staring in

on   the   world
from the outside
asking   to   be
found   on   the
outside asking to
be found from
the   outside
asking   to   be

(it accepts as
an   exist-
ence   the
postulate of
the   lost)

 Have they caught our scent of prescription drugs and support groups?

Someone leans near in the dark and whispers:

Is it a fragrance for them? Is it a p e r e n n i a l ? Are they pricked while we mend?

theirs is the most recent

and probably last replace-ment for e t e r n i t y .'

Can they even count these stitches down to the first zero from which our infinity is d e v i s e d ?

'the missing are the closest thing you have to a soul;

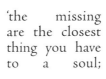

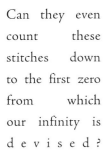 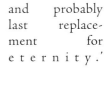 

I turn to see who
is speaking but

there   is   no
one   there

A ▶ ◀ B

FOLD PAGE OVER
LIKE THIS!

A ▶   ◀ B

If all we are is
form, then folding in and folding out defines
the simplest fury of our clipped momentum,
                              and all life is deserted on a list of possible
hiding places for things inside of other things.
God is the unfolding of disbelief's failure
                              to outwit the demand for the infinity
of a larger voice enfolded in bunches of a more
fragile breathing. Death is felt as the folding of
nothing into the paths the present ploughs under,
enclosures surrendered to enclosures, like mind
                              as the first model for incarceration opening
up the possibility for profiles of tortured
mobility, or the belief that the moon
                              is some crazed fire ripped from the sky
on a moonless night and stuffed down
                              the throat of every enemy – until their
only and irreverent gift to the world
                              is the least tangible example of silence for
the far-reaching force of the speaking
few. Love is the faintest feats of hate folding
                              tight around an impossible
adoration for distance. Hate
                              is love folding away from the hope
for some truncated distance, like a poem
as the folding-in fingers which, in closing,
escape their fisty fixity and dissolve into the briefest
                              palm. A poem

A ▶   Fold Back So "A" Meets "B"   ◀ B

PERMISSIONS AND SOURCES

1. The passages from Bush and Debord quoted in "Predicting the Next Big Advertising Breakthrough Using a Potentially Dangerous Method" are found, respectively, at/in: "Address to a Joint Session of Congress and the American People." *The White House: President George W. Bush*. Sept. 2001. The White House. January 2003. ww.whitehouse.gov/news/releases/2001/09/ 20010920-8.html Debord, Guy. *The Society of the Spectacle*. Trans. Donald Nicholson-Smith. New York: Zone, 2002. 18.

2. "Metro" is a trailerization of Pound's "In a Station of the Metro." Pound, Ezra. "In a Station of the Metro." *The Selected Poems of Ezra Pound*. New York: Laughlin, 1949. 35.

3. The Benjamin passage quoted in "1 Epigraph +Five Postcards Addressed by an Admirer to Walter Benjamin Hanging on the Fridge + a Memo on a Napkin (Not Yet Sent)" is taken from: Benjamin, Walter. "Theses on the Philosophy of History." *Illuminations*. 1969. Trans. Harry Zohn. Ed. Hannah Arendt. New York: Schocken, 1988. 255.

4. "Now Dead the Apocalypse" is a grafting of a passage from Brando's "horror" monologue in *Apocalypse Now* with the last paragraph of Joyce's "The Dead." Milius, John, Francis Ford Coppola and Michael Herr. "Kurtz's Monologue." *The Actor's Book of Movie Monologues*. Ed. Marisa Smith and Amy Schewel. New York: Penguin, 1987. 162. Joyce, James. "The Dead." *The Dubliners*. 1914. London: Penguin, 2000. 225.

5. The photo of the author in "Alpino. (2002)" appears with the permission of Michelle Katchuck.

6. The epigraph of "How We Know We Are Being Addressed by the Man Who Shot Himself Online" is quoted from: Rilke, R. M. "Archaic Torso of Apollo." Trans. H. Landman. *Archaic Torso of Apollo*. 4 Apr. 2001/23 July 2003. Howard A. Landman. Feb. 18 2005. www.polyamory.org/~howard/Poetry/rilke_archaic_ apollo.html\

The images in "How . . ." appear with the permission of: "Video of Man at Police Station." No date. Online image. *About Simpleton*. January 2006. http://members.shaw.ca/bankless/.

7. The photo of the author in "Missing" appears with the permission of Barry and Elizabeth Tysdal.

PHOTO: JAYNE TYSDAL

ABOUT THE AUTHOR

DANIEL SCOTT TYSDAL received the John V. Hicks Manuscript Award from the Saskatchewan Writers Guild for *Predicting the Next Big Advertising Breakthrough Using a Potentially Dangerous Method*. It is his first book publication, but his poetry has appeared in a number of Canadian literary journals and has aired on CBC Radio, where he was a finalist in the 2005 National Poetry Face-Off. A poem from this collection, "An Experiment in Form," received an honourable mention at the National Magazine Awards.

Born in Moose Jaw, Daniel Scott Tysdal is completing his Masters Degree studies in English, and has worked as a bartender, grounds-keeper and English teacher. He continues to live in Moose Jaw.